Reviews of Book "A Ne
on Education by Eric Fr

"Eric Frazier, a retired educator and school administrator has poignantly addressed the declining academic performance of students in our public schools nationwide in "A New Educational Paradigm, Perspectives on Education." Increased funding, or "throwing money" at the problem will not unilaterally correct this concern without a Paradigm shift in developing a strategic plan in training teachers, administrators and ancillary professionals. Written during the Covid-19 Pandemic, Mr. Frazier provides information on systemic changes required, in delivering meaningful instructional methods of the "New Normal." This is a read for perspective pedagogues, community leaders and parents who are committed to a belief that a competitive and functioning public school system is a foundation for a true democratic society."

Robert Norris: Retired Principal, Administrator
and Educator; NYC Board of Education;
Boston Public Schools; Cleveland, Board of
Education; Hempstead, NY Public Schools

"The New Educational Paradigm, Perspectives on Education covers a wide range of pedagogy pertinent to urban and rural school systems. It's an easy read and a must read for contemporary educators and students of teacher education."

Ronald Braithwaite, Ph.D.
Senior Research Scientist
Evaluation and Research Associates, Inc.

"As a distinguished and unrelenting educator with an extensive and illustrious career in the Public School System, Eric Frazier is an expert leader. He has designed a paradigm to ensure that there is no "misleadership" nor misalignment in services, resources and support for all students and staff. As the landscape of education continues to change this consummate educator continues to provide support for equity in the various learning communities by focusing on the academic economics, social emotional and political contexts that surround our schools. Frazier continues to uplift our humanity."

Dr Audrey Baker
BA, M.Ed, Ed.D., DHL
Administration /Supervision & Leadership

"Education is always evolving defined by the times and circumstances. A New Educational Paradigm is a must read because COVID-19 has created another definition on what education is and should be. Eric Frazier provides a concise, and to the point guide, with tools for administrators, teachers, college prep educational programs, and governmental agencies on how to prepare all students for success."

Frank Spradley, former Deputy Superintendent,
Principal Benjamin Banneker High School, Principal
Elementary School PS 137. Brooklyn, New York, Leadership
Coach for the New York City Leadership Academy K-12

This book is dedicated to my mom, Marjorie Elizabeth Frazier, who was my first example of an avid reader and a self-made person, with unwavering perseverance and success. She represented my personal perspectives that are contained in the proverbs "There are a thousand ways to skin a cat" in which I added "You just have to find one" and "Obstacles are something you see when you lose sight of the goal."

To my dad who taught me the essence of ambassadorship, the importance of humor, and the enjoyment of life. He taught me how to hustle by stating, "You could always make a dime in New York." I knew then, as a child, I would never go broke.

To my great-grandmother Buma who taught me "God helps those who help themselves!" and "Cleanliness is next to godliness!"

To my aunt Alma who bought me a chemistry set at the age of ten, which inspired me to become a science teacher.

To my brother Ron in heaven, who was my ride-or-die partner, a great artist, athlete, and a family man.

To my sister Linda and cousin Freda in heaven, who will be part of me always.

To my sisters Cheryl, Allison, Nyasa, brother Bill, daughters, and extended family for whom I have tried to be an example.

To my friends who have added invaluable riches to my life.

To my professional friends who inspire me with their contributions for the common good.

To the jazz artists and friends I have had the pleasure of working, performing with, and producing.

To all those who came before us and on whose shoulders we stand.

And, finally, to the children and future generations for whom this work is to benefit.

I am you, and you are me.

Contents

Foreword

have always lauded those who choose education as a career. I think every American should have tremendous gratitude for the selfless sacrifices of those educators and school personnel who endeavor tirelessly to prepare future generations for meaningful roles in society. When I wrote my research-based and national best-seller book, *From Rage to Hope: Strategies for Reclaiming Black and Hispanic Students (2005)*, it was to provide data-driven strategies that educators, administrators, policy makers, parents, and other caring members of the school-home community could put in place to bring out the best in all students. I took great pains in that book to celebrate the contributions and often unheralded impacts of loving "merchants of hope" who choose a career that allows them to make, mold, and touch the future.

I believe every educator has a deep desire to see public schools flourish. Everyone must know that if our children don't succeed, our nation no longer succeeds. Education is one of the social systems that can deliver or destroy a society. I believe the voices of those who have ideas and opinions on how to improve the quality and delivery of educational services should be heard. My passion for education and my desire to encourage opinions and lift the voices of those who also want to see our schools have optimum success and impact led me to accept the invitation to write this foreword. It is the collective genius of educators who want to improve schools that will propel progress and generate the education outcomes most desired by all.

Eric Frazier is such a voice. A long-time educator and native New Yorker, Eric offers his thoughts and perspectives on the need for and implementation of a new educational paradigm. With a strong and passionate appeal to like-minded educators, Eric shares his personal observations and opinions on the education goals and values every school must seek to teach and practice. Perhaps because of his own history as a student and teacher in New York City public schools, he raises the questions and offers his answers on how educators, administrators, and school communities can make schools what they were intended to be. In raising questions, Eric challenges all of us to do more to reap more as he asks, "Who benefits?" and "Who loses?"

Eric's thoughts on how to improve education, in general, are shared with conviction and compassion. He takes the reader on a journey that explores the college education programs for prospective teachers. With his blunt assessment that teaching is not for everyone, Eric offers ideas for a hands-on approach to learning that will allow every educator to have more success. A champion for homeless students and those who have traditionally been undereducated, Eric raises questions about priorities and practices. He seeks to touch the hearts and minds of those who are in position to make a difference, even if it means doing more to reach more.

A realist, Eric also explores the impact of COVID-19 on education in general and in New York City in particular. In sharing his thoughts on environmental factors and the likely use of vaccines for educators and students, Eric offers a realistic view of necessary actions. He discusses what he feels are the requisite components for training education personnel, educational leaders, and those in the hierarchy of education. His thoughts on student "growth" during a pandemic are welcome reminders that we can and must overcome the losses brought about by requisite school closings. He also provides his assessments of community responsibilities and presents his considerations for school openings as educators seek to make up for lost time in the classroom.

The aims of public education require reassessment in light of pressing needs of contemporary learners. In providing his assessments, observations, ideas, and opinions, Eric provokes additional thought from like-minded individuals. Given his emphatic appeal for professional development that will facilitate real improvements in teacher preparation, Eric gives us all food for thought. Everyone has a role to play in preparing students for the challenges of tomorrow. In articulating his thoughts and expressing his appreciation for those in the trenches of education, Eric releases a moving reminder that we are all responsible for what does or does not happen in our schools.

Dr. Crystal Kuykendall, Esq BA, Southern Illinois University; MA, Montclair State University; -EdD education administration Clark-Atlanta University; juris doctor (JD) Georgetown University Law Center; Master of Divinity, Virginia Union University.

Dr. Kuykendall was appointed to the National Advisory Council on Continuing Education by President Carter where she served as council chairperson. She is also president and general counsel of

Kreative and Innovative Resources For Kids Inc., her own firm, and is one of the nation's prominent speakers on the Speakers Circuit.

Preface

This book is, by no means, the definitive end-all to issues confronting educational efficacy and ideology today. It is, however, an attempt to encourage the conversation surrounding educational practices, policies, decision-making, and perspectives.

It is designed to push the narrative on addressing educational concerns in a fashion that, more appropriately, meets the demands of producing outcomes that are suitable and relevant for success among students. It endeavors to call attention to the effectiveness of educational pursuits and their impact on society to bring about the most optimal level of good for all.

Further, the intention of this undertaking is to spotlight the significance of commitment, follow-through, and oversight and to focus on results that are greatly needed to realize the potential of education.

Acknowledgments

M uch thanks to my daughter, Dr. DuEwa M. Frazier, for helping me chart the way forward in this work. Many thanks for contributions to this work to Dr. Audrey Baker, Dr. Gerry Baker, Dr. Victor Gathers, Dr. Crystal Kuykendal, Dr. Gail Reed Barnett, Dr. Ronald Braithwaite, Ms. Deborah Nance, and Ms. Tracey Fuller.

Forty-Six Reasons Why You Should Be Interested in Reading This Book!

You should be interested in reading this book

1. if you have children in school;
2. if you know someone with kids in school;
3. if you want to know more about the pandemic;
4. if you want to know how the pandemic affects education;
5. if you want to know how to improve education;
6. if you want to have better-prepared teachers, administrators, and educational school personnel;
7. if you want to know how to build student achievement;
8. if you want better safety conditions in schools during the pandemic;

9. if you want to know how leadership makes a difference in education;
10. if you want to know what it means to be educated;
11. if you want to know the impact of education on society;
12. if you want to know how to get students more interested in school;
13. if you want to know how new teachers can be trained better;
14. if you want to know how home environments can impact student learning;
15. if you want to know how distant learning versus in-school learning affects your child's education;
16. if you want to know how distant learning affects children with special needs;
17. if you want to know why schools have to close during the pandemic;
18. if you want to know why fewer teachers are working during the pandemic;
19. if you want to know the effects of community spread of the coronavirus on schools and

20. because it demonstrates what we lost sight of in terms of what education is supposed to do, its product, and its impact on society;

21. because it lays out a plan on how to train college students who wish to be prospective teachers and how to monitor their progress three to five years into their careers by evaluating student achievement;

22. because it changes how students are prepared to become teachers by altering college-education curricula to two years liberal arts and last two years in schools physically and virtually;

23. because it talks about retired teachers as trainers and mentors as opposed to in-school training that currently leaves more to be desired;

24. because it changes how all education personnel are trained and evaluated;

25. because it changes leadership emphasis and develops consistent evaluative and oversight processes throughout the levels of education including federal, state, city, and local school districts;

26. because it discusses the impact of the coronavirus pandemic on education in detail;

27. because it discusses the efficacy of pandemic vaccines as it relates to education;
28. because it reinforces the value of education;
29. because it discusses the impact of education on every aspect of society;
30. because it adds services and personnel to schools that help aid parenting;
31. because it discusses a plan for helping students with psychological and mental stress situations;
32. because it lays out a realistic set of ideas regarding students going back to school in a pandemic environment;
33. because it discusses the effectiveness of hybrid learning versus traditional learning;
34. because it talks about educated people versus people who are trained;
35. because it is a book whose information we can no longer do without;
36. because it is timely and very much needed;
37. because the information is organized and succinct;
38. because it advocates for the proper status of teachers in our society;
39. because the topics are hot, and it is what grabs the interest of people these days;

40. because there are groups of educators, book clubs, media, friends, and TV and radio people anticipating its release;

41. because it's an encouragement for people locked inside due to the pandemic;

42. because a jazz artist (www.ericfraziermusic.com) wrote this book as a way of making good use of time and a way of giving while there were no gigs during the pandemic;

43. because it's an inspirational idea for searching souls;

44. because it is the author's expertise as a former educational executive;

45. because the author has a radio station on Pandora.com and a TV show *Cultural Spectrums and Jazz Pearls* (google)—both of which are helpful in pushing the narrative; and

46. because it speaks truth to power and puts decision-makers and implementers on notice.

It is for the above reasons and more that you should read this book.

CHAPTER 1

Values of Education

> People you thought were edu-
> cated were trained and not
> educated!
>
> —Eric Frazier

There are those who are trained and those who are educated. What is the difference, and to what extent are we actually an educated people? Is there a criterion that can allow us to explain and quantify this quandary?

First, we can agree that a trained person is someone who has acquired skills which are necessary to do a particular job or fill a specific role. It may not be essential to utilize those skills outside of that role and therefore require any incentive to take into consideration their impact on other factors. One follows a recipe to be utilized no matter the situation, and the other uses various situations to dictate the course of action. Even though we are among the highly educated societies of the world, we are still lacking in producing the potential we aspire in our people. Endeavors to enhance our educational goals and objectives have lagged behind our need for desired growth and prosperity.

Years ago, at least in New York City, there was an attempt at establishing a criterion that could have possibly been considered as a part of the production function of education (see chapter 12 "Aims and Objectives of Public Education in New York City). It delineated the goals of education whereby the outcomes in the type and, to some extent, quality of people produced in the system could be measured or verified as its product. The actual characteristics of students completing high school or college would be a representation of fundamental values produced in people as a result of education. It could very well be one of the reasons why achievement levels on academic tests vary indirectly with character traits of people going into various careers. It is understood that these are values in which to aspire. Please note that such concerns have remained as an albatross on our shoulders since those who started our country were banned from England. These issues have evolved to permeate systems throughout society from which we have yet to recover. Therein lies the relevance of education as a modicum of balancing how we will function together in society. It is distinctly my perspective that examples of some of the characteristic value traits that can be acquired from study in education are as follows:

A value and appreciation for the following:

Learning
Exploration
Research
Discovery
Innovation

A value and appreciation for the following:

Study
Scholarship
Lifelong Learning
Education
Academics including math, social studies, current events, history, science, languages, reading, literature, writing, etc.
Technology

Public speaking
Language
Nature and ecological relationships
Economics and economic relationships
The arts including music, dance, theater, painting, sculpture, etc.
Aesthetics and aesthetic relationships
Home economics
Physical education
Health and health education
Sex education
Special education
Career skills and career education
Government
Citizenship
Community
Neighborhood
Family
Service to others
Good judgment
Decision-making
Intuitive and cognitive thinking
Organization
Growth and development
Relationships—personal, social, group,
Culture

Appreciation for cultures of others
Appreciation for diversity
Working well with others
Human nature
Focus and concentration
Understanding and respecting various points of views
Balance
Inquiry
Knowledge
Physical fitness

A value and appreciation for the following:

Teamwork
Leadership
Initiative
Work ethic
Integrity
Positivity
Respect
Honor
Love
Manners

A value and appreciation for the following:

Seeing a task through to its completion
Understanding
Listening
Conversation
Creative endeavors
Careers
Invention

These values relate to some of the traits that may be readily identified in persons produced through an effective educational system to greater or lesser degrees. They are values which amount to fundamental behaviors and skills that can be universally recognized and appropriately projected as examples of student attributes in a system that is accountable for its product. This is a representative list, and by no means is it exhaustive. They, in effect, are ideals to be realized in each and every student. Additionally, these values amount to factors that can be viewed as components that help us arrive at the question, What inputs are needed to reach the desired educational outcomes? (Economically speaking, what then would be the production function of education?) This formula and calculation require much more than meets the eye in a glance. It is not as cut-and-dry as in business where if you put in x amount of inputs, you will be able to calculate y amounts of output. It is why in the chapters that follow, we will aspire to unravel a multitude of elements that go into the arrival of what ought to be considered in constructing an educational model for future generations.

CHAPTER 2

Alternatives to Traditional Preparation
of Prospective Teachers and
Systemwide Policy Decision-Making

The education system was not only designed to enhance the knowledge base and skills of those entering the world of work in its many changing facets but it also stood as a fitting vehicle for migrating from other countries to assimilate into the fabric of cultural norms, traditions, and values of the American society. The educational process served to facilitate the efforts of immigrants in becoming productive citizens. It is, parenthetically, one of the most singularly important reasons why America is great. It also cannot go without mention that the advent of Slavery and free labor and it's aid in helping to establish multiple colleges, universities, businesses, patents and inventions, unethically emanating from slaves, is another reason however dark, why America is great.

Let us fast-forward to the status of education in America today. It is common knowledge that high school dropout rates, inconsistent school attendance, and inadequate levels of achievement plague school profiles nationally. In general, student interest in school activities calls for more reasons to build excitement surrounding the learning environment, with more creative ways to heighten educational appeal.

Schools have the opportunity to be the most fascinating places and laboratories for growth and human development for students. What would preclude such good from taking place?

Does the product we offer tell them that we don't really care? Is it that we just want it to look like we care? Is this the message students get? Obviously, we need to alter our priorities. We are currently experiencing a time when the efficacy of our institutions is in grave question. Who are these institutions serving, and to what end? Who stands to benefit, and who loses out? How can change help ameliorate these issues within the institution of education?

Let us not be absorbed by status quo features but rather engaged more with focus on the advancement of educational pursuits.

First, let us note that there is a dire need for schools, in general, to have a more significant relationship to jobs in terms of facilitating job placements and internships right out of high school or college. A stronger link between business and government to facilitate this matter is indeed applicable. Second, it would be helpful to have that link expanded to address the need for businesses, corporations, private industry, and government to establish a vehicle to pay for student college expenses. The establishment of internships during or after completing high school would be a great way of enhancing the potential for success of individuals and organizations. Internships serve to help build the skill level and knowledge base of entry-level workers, while increasing the potential for efficiency, productivity and the economic strength of our economy. It is something that would undeniably add to the notion of "building back better," utilizing our greatest resource, which is the people. Similarly, scholarships, sponsorships, and fellowships are avenues in which businesses, corporations, private industry, and government can play significant roles in helping drive the education narrative. Hopefully, these ideas and more will be significant priorities placed on the agenda of the new secretary of education in the President Biden administration.

Let's discuss prospective teachers and college education. Why is it necessary for college students who aspire to be teachers to spend four years in the college itself? Two years of liberal-arts courses will serve to afford them a rounded and balanced experience of the academic and societal perspectives. It may serve society better to have prospective student teachers learn their craft at school locations. COVID-19 considerations and new technologies of virtual distance learning at their homes or college settings with professorial guidance and retiree mentorship would facilitate student preparation. This gives them a chance to learn virtual-lesson strategies from proven masters and allows them to understand how to function in a school environment that also encompasses hybrid learning modalities. Teaching is not for everyone, and everyone is not necessarily cut out to be a teacher. Also, those looking to go into the teaching profession would have an opportunity to find out if teaching is something they really want to pursue. Prospective teachers would have an opportunity to learn the craft in theory and in practice. Essentially, schedules could be established, which gives students courses that summarily amount to field-study endeavors. Learning under college professors in a field-study format that is set up to make use of control groups would necessarily facilitate a clinical approach. The benefit of this methodology would give students a hands-on experience while providing a vehicle for enabling the assessment of their progress and growth. This, of course, would be diametrically opposed to the traditional four-year-in-class theory courses. It would make for an enormous value with great promise and a better fit for a more prepared teaching corp. Its potential impact on student learning and student achievement would go a long way toward building an effective teaching population. Such a plan, to prepare prospective teachers who are in college, would call for the two years of field study and three years of mentorship and professional training required to extract desired outcomes in the achievement of classroom students. It has the potential to translate to a pronounced increase in student achievement and test scores as well as on the overall academic success of students within their midst.

Additionally, experienced retired-teacher trainers with proven track records of success in special and general education would be on board to train at timely sessions in the schools or through virtually distanced training. Teacher trainers would also have the ability to be involved as on-site mentors serving as liaisons between the school organization and the college. This would help resolve the issue of inadequate time for training and of using school personnel to train, who also have multiple other duties to address. College students would be taught such things as how to structure and plan lessons; how to use student experiences to motivate or build interest for lessons; how to deliver, conclude, and follow up lessons; and also how to be a good coach and source of motivation. Prospective teachers in this scenario would also learn how to interact with students, colleagues, parents and community, supervisors, guidance counselors, and other school personnel. These activities would take place within the last two years of college. Under this program, which I will entitle the New Educational Paradigm Future Teachers Corp, schools would benefit by getting prospective teachers who are prepared and better trained. Students would also profit by receiving an improved level of instruction and greater chances for increased student performance. The assessment processes for growth in achievement of children taught by teachers in this program would infinitely provide a built-in method for programmatic success. Training should be ongoing throughout the first three years of professional service. This effectively outsources teacher training and leaves only those details particular to individual schools for teachers to absorb. Progress of these endeavors should then be reported daily to principals as needed. This scenario gives timely help to solving problems connected with school personnel decision-making, filling vacancies, and attracting quality teachers. It has been said that teachers are the single most significant factor in a student's education. It therefore behooves us to invest appropriately in their preparation. Additionally, remember that it is teachers who are charged with the responsibility of educating everyone in our society. How would we function without them? How is it possible that they are not paid commensurate to their role in making the entire society work?

CHAPTER 3

Impact of the Coronavirus
Pandemic on Education

The COVID-19 pandemic takes a distinct presence in this discussion due to its extensive role in influencing our national health, well-being and the proliferation of life in America. The mere magnitude and expansiveness of the rate of its implacable force challenge the mind and change indefinitely the way we live in the world today. The adverse effects it has levied on various systems, including government, private industry, and corporations in general and education in particular, have warranted unprecedented reactions. The extent of irrational thinking and behavior surrounding this pandemic crisis has been unmatched by any standard in our history.

Prior to the newly elected team of, President Joe Biden and Vice President Kamala Harris, we witnessed the United States as a country that was disjointed, disorganized, and confused regarding a concerted approach to the pandemic. This situation was due, in large part, to a lack of leadership and a national plan for addressing the coronavirus pandemic under the previous President Donald Trump's administration. Does anyone actually plan to fail? It's what happens when you fail to plan. Please note that one of the most fundamental axioms in theory of organizations, whether in government, private business, or anywhere else, is that leadership dictates success particularly when obstacles or challenges arise.

During the current COVID-19 pandemic, a number of factors have immerged significantly. Many teachers and educators were of the view that it was too dangerous to take a chance returning to school and that their lives and the safety of their families and their students would hang in the balance. We have experienced a lost in the number of educators available to serve students. You could well imagine the type of impact this situation would have on the entire educational system. Additionally, of the teachers who did return, what changed in their behalf and the behalf of students regarding procedures governing those contracting the disease, quarantining, students with discipline problems, homelessness, health obstacles, poverty, and students with special needs? These areas will need more attention and hopefully will be adequately addressed by the time this book is published.

Consider these factors in addressing the most substantial health crisis we face today in society and particularly in education, in our lifetime:

First, note that more teachers are needed than ever to fill vacancies due to guidelines for social distancing and smaller class sizes. Similarly, more guidance counselors and custodial workers are required to address social/psychological issues, PPE inventory, and school cleaning needs respectively. Since distance learning is required in some instances, many students in disadvantage neighborhoods are without the necessary technology to receive lessons, particularly those who are handicapped and who require an aide to assist them in utilizing an iPad or other technical equipment. Homeless students are acutely vulnerable in this situation. In many cases, students do not use the same iPad during each class or change of class. Some schools store iPads or other essential technical equipment for students in case of deficient devices or in the event that students simply do not have a device. This leads to changing hands of materials without proper disinfecting precautions. Apparently, these issues are still not appropriately addressed, and children are sent to schools regardless of the extent, incidence, and thoroughness of implementation of essential activities.

Additionally, we know that the coronavirus is airborne and can remain in the air for hours at a time. Schools located in the cities are particularly vulnerable due to the air quality which may contain pollutants such as mercury, carbon monoxide, and more, that contribute to the spread of the virus. These areas are generally most populated by Black and Brown students. Research conducted by the International Journal of Environmental Research and Public Health has shown that the coronavirus had been detected in air pollution (called particulate matter) enabling the virus to travel much farther than previously suspected, up to more than thirty feet!

The coronavirus pandemic is having an adverse effect on the economy, which affects not only funding for schools but also the entire gamut of societal well-being including jobs, health, consumer activity and more. Economists such as Kevin Hassett, former chairman of the Council of Economic Advisers and senior adviser of President Trump, predicted that economic recovery would take about eight to ten years and that the virus would play a large role in the length of the recovery. The coronavirus was brought to New York from Europe, which was contrary to original thinking that asserted its derivation was from China. It was detected during the month of February 2020 and tracked during the spread. The close down of schools began in New York after a brief reopening in late September. Schools were again shut down due to the increased spread of COVID-19 cases during the second wave of the pandemic, only to be partly reopened on the second week of December 2020. That amounts to almost eight months of learning lost due to instructional inconsistencies brought on by the COVID-19 pandemic. It presented a less than enviable challenge to the continuity of learning that is needed to compound knowledge and information essential for educational growth and heightened achievement levels. It is quite likely that this loss of learning may never be made up unless the school year is expanded to a twelve-month operation, the school day is extended, or an additional year is added, which would make school study through high school a thirteen-year proposition as opposed to the current twelve-year status.

On December 21, 2020, Mayor de Blasio of New York introduced a digital education plan to make up for educational losses due to the present COVID-19 pandemic. The plan was designed to bring students current with the learning that was lost. Its purpose was to close the achievement gap for students, in general, with digital programs for each individual student's learning and to have the program in place by September 2021. Individual digital programs similar to the concept developed for special-education students as part of their IEPs (individualized education programs) would be a huge advantage for all students.

During his daily update on January 14, 2021, on this topic, Mayor de Blasio announced that in addition to innovations regarding digitalized instruction to make up for lost learning, there would be a focus on learning inequalities and disparities associated with neighborhoods of Black and Brown students. He mentioned that these measures would be implemented in order to close the achievement gap for September 2021. He also brought up the fact that 247 out of the 869 schools in New York City were opened five days per week. The rest of the schools were engaged in hybrid learning (combination of distance learning and in-school learning) and virtual distance learning only. These processes exemplified the breath of complicated decisions that had to come to fruition in real time. There were time constraints, health parameters, physical limitations, and location structural considerations that needed to be taken into account. The factors were all reliant on funding and the cooperation of stakeholders in order to realize the desired goals and objectives.

Obviously, this predicament creates a devastating impact on students who are endeavoring to get through schooling and enter college or the world of work. It also leaves to question testing outcomes and evaluation of student growth in an ill-functioning school situation. On what basis will statewide and citywide end of year and midyear testing be effective? How will student-achievement measures be able to give accurate assessments of student success? A planning team established to address these topics and more regarding educational issues is required so that from the highest level of the educational chain to the service level in schools, everyone is on the same page regarding goals, objectives, and systemic oversight.

There is a plethora of coronavirus test kits on the market. However, at the time of this writing, some have been unreliable, and some also did not have Food and Drug Administration approval. (You will, no doubt, receive more information about recent news of home coronavirus testing kits, which are said to have 100 percent accuracy). Contact tracing is a key component of this process due to the fact that it follows the spread of the virus from one person to another and attempts to locate the original spreader. It allows for information to be accrued related to the extent of the spread and, to some degree, the rate of the spread. It is therefore essential to controlling the spread in schools and communities. Dr. Peter Hotez, director of the Texas Children's Hospital Center for Vaccine Development, stated that "the COVID-19 impact, besides apparent deaths, may include long term injury to the lungs, heart, vascular system, neurological deficits and cognitive deficits which could plague the country even years after vaccines will be discovered." Consider the aforementioned statement along with the idea that there is a significant lack of research regarding long-term problems of COVID-19 survivors. Taking such medical affirmations into account, is there even a small wonder why there should not be a wholesale rush to place our children and vital workers into harm's way? Some would say there is a saving grace in that more people are surviving now than in the initial onslaught of the disease. We know more about the illness now, and that could be reason for more survivors. Others would say we have more fatalities than ever before, and the spread is much quicker. However, even though both points of view have legitimate roots, the need for speed in getting the virus under control remains a footrace in getting out ahead of the spread. It puts a focus on vaccine distribution and the time it takes for it to even matter.

CHAPTER 4

Environmental Factors
Surrounding Safety in Schools

U nfortunately, until the recent administration—President Biden, Vice President Harris—came into office, handling the pandemic was about managing ignorance on a national scale. There was still a wide range of people who did not believe the coronavirus was as lethal as it was purported to be. This included Donald Trump, the president of the United States, who also contracted the virus along with members of his staff. He threatened to cut funds for schools refusing to reopen through the midst of the first wave of the pandemic during the summer of 2020! This approach was antithetical to warnings of the American Academy of Pediatrics regarding endangering the health of our children during the high rates of infection taking place across the country. It was simply common sense. North Dakota hospitals were experiencing nearly 100 percent capacity during the midst of the second wave of the COVID-19 pandemic. *Grand Forks Herald* newspaper reported that the governor of the state, Doug Burgum, announced that nurses who contracted the disease could continue working. Evidently, that decision epitomized the mentality surrounding this issue on the highest of levels in many areas.

Reopening of schools is still an issue that calls for monitoring on a continual basis. Schools in New York were opened during the end of September and closed again in the middle of November due to another increase of the virus during the second wave of the pandemic. Since New York was the first state to experience the widespread devastation of the virus, its handling of the disease, under Governor Cuomo, became the prototype for cities throughout the nation. New York brought its positivity rate down to 1.1 percent (the lowest in the country at the time of this writing) and its deaths to zero in some instances. However, it was and still is not without significant problems that other cities will, no doubt, have to confront as well. During the second wave of spiked positivity rates across the country, rates increased to double digits in New York and well over double digits in other places countrywide (30 percent in California, almost three out of every ten people, and nearly 56 percent in South Dakota, more than one out of every two people). Double-digit rates were actually commonplace throughout much of the country. It was established in New York City schools that there would be a total shutdown upon reaching a 3 percent or above positivity rate. There have been discussions surrounding the identification of school clusters where certain schools could be closed and not the entire system depending on positivity rates of areas which housed the schools. The problem would arise as to the extent of trafficking in areas from other localities in an attempt to control the spread of the virus.

The New York City Council of School Supervisors and Administrators called for the State Department of Education to oversee the supervision of the reopening of schools due to repeated mistakes and miscalculations taking place in trying to open schools for the end of September 2020 on the local level. They cited problems of staff shortages due to blended learning (in class and virtual distance learning) and smaller class sizes, which required a need for more teachers and support staff, as some examples. Additionally, principals were being pressured by school superintendents to say schools were ready for reopening when that was simply not the case.

Also, the teachers' union wanted distance learning to be taught from home, while the Department of Education wanted it taught from the school setting. These are issues that will occur in just about any school setting in cities of America. Their resolution will call for experimental initiatives that ensure safety first. However, additional questions still remain, such as the incidence of random testing, how often it will take place, and whether it's even happening at all! The rate of disinfecting activity and how often it can be done safely are certainly huge questions.

A 3 percent infection rate is a red flag, and a 5 percent infection rate is a signal that schools must close in New York City. The state required school closings at 9 percent during that time. The importance of being on the same page in this instance could not be overstated.

The pandemic has also served greatly to continue to expose issues of Black Lives Matter, immigration, economy, racism, LGBT, and other matters associated with institutional and systemwide operations that were heretofore not made more relevant to the lives of everyday people. These issues, no doubt, permeated the home environments of students engaged in schooling, which, in turn, placed unintended stresses on children. How can the damage to their home or in-school learning situations be measured?

During the COVID-19 spread across the country, some states were closing down not only schools but also the entire state. The template for addressing the coronavirus developed by New York has shown that whole-state closedowns were unnecessary. It was stated by the governor of New York that it was paramount to identify regions that had micro clusters of the virus through contact tracing. He stated, "The procedure was to close those areas off to test and quarantine the people and then retest to control the spread." Obviously, dense areas, such as cities, are more susceptible than less-populated areas, and that is precisely why city schools were more at risk. In Governor Cuomo's public briefing on October 22, 2020, he cited the issues and points such as the fact that additional spread of the virus was caused by lack of compliance and enforcement on the local level and that communities must respond in kind to control the spread. During the second wave of the coronavirus pandemic, New York City was labeled an orange zone by the state, which meant that houses of worship could have 33 percent capacity with twenty-five people maximum, mass gatherings indoor and outdoor could have ten people maximum, high-risk nonessential businesses such as gyms and personal care should be closed, outdoor dining could have four persons maximum per table, and schools with remote learning were required to have students test negative in order for school districts to reopen. It was asserted that a $1,000 fine would be imposed on violators of COVID-19 rules and that schools would reopen increasingly depending on the success of various areas in decreasing the rate of the spread of the virus.

The remaining color zones explained by Governor Cuomo also contained rules by which adherence was required. The yellow zone called for positivity rates of 2.5 percent. Rules included houses-of-worship capacity of 50 percent, mass gatherings with twenty-five people maximum, opening of businesses, dining indoor/outdoor with four people maximum per table, and opening of schools with mandatory 20 percent testing.

The red zone called for positivity rates of 3 percent. Rules included houses-of-worship capacity of 25 percent with ten people maximum, prohibited mass gatherings, essential businesses only, takeout and delivery only, and schools having remote learning and "testing out" to open.

The essence of those initiatives was that a plan was established; the most fundamental quality of which was the implementation and oversight, that remained as an example to be replicated by other areas. The plan allowed for a way to address the unabated spread of COVID-19 so that it did not continue to run amok without being managed.

Additionally, there was an issue regarding children and students entering the New York City school system for the first time and the required immunization vaccinations. How was this process to be accomplished given the existing overwhelming medical preoccupation with the coronavirus disease? This may change, but right now, it is alarming.

In general, forty million coronavirus vaccinations were needed in the state of New York. Questions arose as to how they were to be administered and what would be the priority for who received the vaccinations first. People were skeptical about the vaccines and did not want be guinea pigs for the endeavor, particularly among Black and Brown Americans who have endured a history of detrimental medical experiments that reflected little or no concern for their lives and their health. They will need to be assured their safety in getting the shots and be ready to come back again in twenty-one days between vaccinations for the Pfizer vaccine or twenty-eight days for the Moderna vaccine. Evidently, this has become a monumental endeavor! It was stated in Cuomo's briefing that three hundred million doses would be needed for the American people, and a logistical operational plan on just how vaccine shots could be administered would need to be established. This was just one of a multitude of questions posed to the federal government by the National Governors Association as stated by Governor Cuomo.

Another influential factor mentioned in the governor's briefing was the cost to our children, their parents, and society of the presence of post-traumatic stress disorder due to COVID-19, which has not even begun to be calculated. This, of course, remains as a factor that we cannot afford to go unaddressed.

Furthermore, as the initial epicenter of the coronavirus in the United States, the entire state of New York was obligated to get on top of the pandemic quickly. Given the absence of leadership on the national level, this became a nightmare of a task for states, cities, and counties in America. Regarding COVID-19 testing, Mayor De Blasio of New York reported that in city schools, out of the sixteen thousand students tested, twenty-eight came out positive, which amounted to a COVID-19 positivity rate of

0.1 percent during October 2020. Parenthetically, in his debriefing to the public, the mayor and his wife, Chirlane McCray, introduced a program of trauma-informed group therapy to support students' mental health in city schools. It was launched in thirty-six schools of which twenty-six had the capacity to refer students to professional services at the time of this writing. (Note in particular the leadership initiatives, the innovations, and the communication process instituted in implementing this plan of action. It is a significant and recurring theme we will visit throughout this conversation.) The psychological impact of children being kept away from their grandparents, being kept indoors and away from friends, experiencing the illness in their families, and witnessing deaths in some cases is absolutely devastating and overwhelming. This is yet another example of the residual litany of obstacles to learning brought on by the pandemic.

CHAPTER 5

Vaccines and Their Potential to Address a Positive Outcome to Control Coronavirus Spread

L et us note at the outset that currently (during the time of this writing), there is no research regarding the study of vaccinations for children. Keep in mind that the coronavirus pandemic has caused more affliction and mortalities than any outbreak of diseases we have witnessed in our lifetime. Further, we have witnessed a presidential campaign, election, and installation of a new president all at the same time of having the highest number of coronavirus disease and casualties since the pandemic began. This has all taken place still without a national plan to control the pandemic. Hence, the country was given a chance to take a sigh of relief upon hearing the announcement of new president-elect Joe Biden along with Vice President Kamala Harris on

November 4, 2020. President Biden announced that he will immediately convene a task force to establish a plan to control the pandemic. It marked the first time during this scourge that a national plan to combat the coronavirus pandemic was introduced.

Accordingly, it should also be noted that on November 9, 2020, the Pfizer company announced that it had produced a coronavirus vaccine with 94.5 percent success rate. Shortly after, on November 17, the Moderna Therapeutics announced they had completed phase 3 of their research trail for the development of a coronavirus vaccine. Phase 3 represented the final stage of research, where thousands of people were tested to ascertain that the vaccine actually worked. Similarly, Moderna affirmed that their vaccine worked with 94.5 percent accuracy with no significant safety concerns. Moderna found success by injecting messenger RNA cells into the body to create antibodies, which support the immune system in fighting off the virus, instead of injecting live virus. This is similar to the way in which the Pfizer vaccine worked and antithetical to how other previous vaccines were said to work by injecting the coronavirus itself to create immunities. Obviously, that would have amounted to quite a problematic way to move forward. It was revealed that MRNA cells attach to the protein spikes of the virus with a film covering to facilitate its entry to DNA cells. There are twenty-nine types of protein in the virus; only one, the spike, is used in the vaccines mentioned and not the entire virus. When the MRNA cells (which imitate but are not actually the virus) enter cells in the body, they reproduce the messenger RNA cells, which are then recognized by T cells in the immune system. The T cells then activate B cells, which obliterate the spikes that are characterized by the coronavirus. If the body is ever exposed to the virus again, it will be recognized in the immune system by T cells and consequently destroyed by B cells. This is the basis of the immunity protocol (based on research from Chemical Abstracts Services, a division of the American Chemical Society).

The differences in the case of the Moderna and Pfizer vaccines were the room temperature at which the vaccines had to be stored. The Moderna vaccine does not require temperatures below zero and could be stored at room temperature whereas the Pfizer vaccine necessitated minus 77 to minus 100 degrees storage. Current lab refrigerators can already accommodate Moderna vaccines, which will facilitate the vaccine distribution, not so for the Pfizer vaccine. In which case, appropriate refrigerators are being developed for the distribution phase, which is currently in progress.

Also, the Pfizer vaccine requires two vaccinations, now twenty-one days apart, while the Moderna vaccine calls for two vaccines, twenty-eight days apart. The amount of protection between doses for both vaccines has not been fully determined at this juncture. Additionally, the length of time the vaccines supported immunity was still in question at the time of this writing. However, new developments have been fast and furious. Apparently, the implications of these declarations are a game changer that will have a bearing on control of the spread of the coronavirus while the pandemic continues. Ostensibly, these developments will have a clear impact on the entire society as well as the aggregate of world health.

A new vaccine was again introduced on November 22 by AstraZeneca Pharmaceuticals, which was said to be cheaper and require normal refrigeration. It also reported a conglomerate 90 percent efficiency rate. AstraZeneca originally gave the wrong dosage to volunteers in their phase 3 testing and had to call off experimentation with the vaccine until the appropriate dosage could be achieved. However, potential drawbacks were exposed, revealing AstraZeneca and Johnson & Johnson's alleged use of adenoviruses as vectors (Ad5 vector) that have been known to induce the probability of attracting the HIV virus and other infections as stipulated by researchers in *The Lancet*, a medical journal, on their November 2020 issue. It is more than likely that this issue will be addressed well before their vaccine goes up for approval with the Food and Drug Administration (FDA).

Vaccine Efficacy

We can be more definitive regarding the effects and importance of vaccines with children. Are the vaccines necessary for them? Our focus has been centered more on young adults and adults, particularly regarding vaccine injections. Questions as to the extent of any side effects or lingering effects of the vaccines remain. Pfizer Company in England led the way for the first vaccine distributions and vaccinations in the world. On December 8, 2020, the first vaccinations took place. Dr. Kavita Patel, former health policy adviser in the President Obama administration and an infectious-disease expert, mentioned potential side effects regarding the efficacy of the vaccines. She asserted that, generally, one could experience soreness, fever, and aches, similar to the flu shots but stronger and also similar to the shingles vaccine but milder. Additionally, Dr. Patel stated that "some reactions could potentially include Bell's palsy, a facial-nerve paralysis that took place in a small number of cases [5 out of 77,000 tested]." She related that "those having a compromised immune status and patients with comorbidity situations, such as heart disease, diabetes, obesity, pregnancy, allergies, and even women who became pregnant between shots, would be at particular risk for potential after-effects." These factors play a substantial role in the health status of school-age children because it is their parents, grandparents, or other family members that would be affected.

Additionally, new mutated variant strains of the coronavirus have been discovered, which were said to spread 70 percent quicker and to be more easily transmitted. The first new strain, which was identified in England on December 18, 2020, was followed by a series of new strains from South Africa, Denmark, Australia, and Brazil. The spread also went to Canada. The first case identified in the United States took place in Colorado on or around December 23, 2020, and had since spread to California and New York, which saw its first case on January 4, 2021. Other states are, no doubt, experiencing the trauma of this new strain as we speak. The South African version is said to cause more disease in young adults ages twenty to thirty. It is not known how susceptible current vaccines are to immunization of these strains. Scientists are of the opinion that vaccines in use may also be sufficient for the new strains. Pfizer researchers in conjunction with the University of Texas medical team found that the new strains were located on the spike of the coronavirus, which is the area that is attacked and destroyed by B cells of the immune system. That is the basis of why they feel current vaccines will work on the new strains to this point. (However, please note that there may be strains that behave differently.) The clinical trials of vaccines such as Pfizer and Moderna have taken place in less than three months (as compared to past clinical trials for vaccines that have taken place over several years). The nature of the answer to how long a durable immune response to the coronavirus may last is parenthetically unknown, and whether vaccine shots will need to occur annually is still to be decided.

Consider also that as of December 31, 2020, Pfizer announced that it would be extending the time between its first and second vaccination shots from twenty-one days to twelve weeks or eighty-four days in order to provide as many first shots to patients as possible. Basically, you will be able to surmise whether this is a shift to an economic emphasis as opposed to a legitimate health concern or both. They have foregone second vaccination shot storage in favor of utilizing available supplies to add to the implementation of first vaccination shots. It may appear that Pfizer is attempting to corner as much of the market as possible without health considerations of those waiting eighty-four days for second shots (However, Pfizer has not followed through with the eighty-four day extension). Getting as many first-shot vaccines out as possible should be a priority. We are experiencing a race against time. Real-time decisions have heavy implications for everyone, especially those having children in our school system. The extent of vulnerability between the first and second vaccinations was not known, nor was the length of time of immunity known after either shot during the time of this writing.

Couple these findings with the fact that as of December 30, 2020, two million people were vaccinated of the twenty million forecasted for this date by the Operation Warp Speed. (Operation Warp Speed is a conglomeration of government agencies and industry charged with delivering 300 million doses of vaccines by January 2021.) Operation Warp

Speed predicted that it would take ten years to vaccinate the number of people needed to stop the spread of the coronavirus at this rate.

Apparently, there were enough unknowns of the research on this topic to construe that it is inconclusive. In the coming months, we shall have an opportunity to discover, in real time, the value of these astonishing revelations and their impact on the process of education in particular and the society in general.

CHAPTER 6

A Systemwide Look at Training Educational Personnel

The COVID-19 environment has exposed inefficiencies, inequities, and incompetency in our systems as a whole. The field of education was not excluded from this reality. There will, undoubtedly, be a change in the way school programs are funded. These ensuing suggestions call for that change. Also suggested are pathways provided for particularly talented retired professionals to be on board for training not only teachers but also the gamut of school personnel charged with educational service to students. This includes teaching assistants, paraprofessionals, guidance counselors, special-education personnel, librarians, substitute teachers, custodians, school security officers, deans, pupil-personnel coordinators, test coordinators, cafeteria heads and workers, school nurses, crossing guards, secretaries, aides, administrators, and supervisors. Also included in this scenario would be training in school business administration with scheduling and programming of classes, assessing and ordering resources and materials, budgeting fund allocations and finance, community outreach, adult education, grant writing, and professional development for all supportive personnel involved. How much training for various roles in the school is to be outsourced and how much should be in-house should depend on the level of need demonstrated by each school. A prominent viewpoint may be to have training similarly across the board. Initially, all schools should require an evaluation on this account.

Inevitably, this would impact the changing role of the Department of Education to one that is more responsive to schools and less autocratic, creating less unnecessary micromanagement and putting in place proven outstanding professionals at every level. Responsiveness to schools is a two-way street. It facilitates needed communication that more adeptly places levels of the service on the same page. It serves to diminish the need for top-heavy central board administrators, who oftentimes are without the experience of school-based personnel. It directs funds toward a program that incorporates gifted retired personnel and prevents the lack of knowledge and experience exodus that leaves when they leave.

It also places worth on the notion that older societies have always treasured—the value of elders as a fountain of wisdom and experience. It calls for a new look at how federal state and local funding are administrated toward education on the service level to enhance inputs designed to directly affect student achievement.

Teachers are vital to the national health, welfare, and interest of our country and should therefore be viewed as such. Having a duly educated society ultimately makes for a happier, healthier, and more competent and stable culture. It also serves to place us appropriately in the worldview regarding the pursuit of good. The days of "Do what we say but not as we do" are long gone. These are times of modeling what we all should do. It is concomitantly why it is suggested that those going into the field of teaching receive scholarships for undergraduate and graduate degrees and that those currently with outstanding loans receive forgiveness.

Implementing the ideas set forth in this discussion would call for such endeavors as establishing a task force to facilitate planning, coordination, research, and feasibility of creating a smooth run of activities. It would require setting resources for funding, staffing, technology, structures, policies, decision-making, accountability, oversight, and services to the community and, ultimately and significantly, to students. Such a planning team would do well to consist of significant representatives of the various levels of service to education, including federal, state, and city along with community, education administrator, teacher, and student delegates.

The establishment of control groups that maintain the status quo against an experimental group of students who wish to study to become teachers will serve to weigh efficacy of a plan to better prepare prospective teachers for careers in the field. Monitoring the progress of an experimental group of students over time would inevitably dictate the value of this type of endeavor. This concept will inevitably be revisited in upcoming segments of this discussion. It is significant to note that such change is the operable factor in the equation for an educational production function. Need is always a driving force. It is what sets the stage for alternate perspectives, genius innovations, and new realities. The well-being of our children, our citizens, and our society depends on our diligence.

However, none of the above would be able to take place without leadership from the very top. It is well understood that education is the responsibility of states. The wedge in this situation comes into play where the federal government and state entities have diametrically opposed agendas, which are more both connected to political affiliations than they are to education and local communities at large. This can only change when the country's chief executive, president, assumes the unprecedented role as the "education president." The president has the ability to convene a committee or task force of the association of governors to put into motion planning that would set guidelines for how effective educational processes could be inculcated into statewide systems. Prevalent among goals and objectives would obviously involve focus on keeping at the forefront oversight necessary up and down the various educational levels to address and provide remedies for issues.

CHAPTER 7

Training Educational Leaders and the Hierarchy of Education

I f there is to be significant change in our educational system, then there will need to be a concrete commitment from the very top. We are talking about an executive commitment from the national government to make decisions that put into motion the leadership, support, and resources to finally make education work for everyone. This commitment would establish education as a priority backed by federal, state, and city funding and would therefore enable the secretary of education to have a more suitable role in providing support for funding and resource allocation to states whose role is to preside over the delivery of education. Changing the position of the secretary of education to a career appointment as opposed to a political appointment is, of course, paramount. It takes politics out of the educational equation and allows for gifted and talented professionals who arise from the ranks with experience and proven success at the service level to assume leadership. Such a leader would undoubtedly have the ability to provide the insight, have continuity of experience, and know how to put essential change into effect. Similar procedures regarding the selection and ascendance of career professionals and the abolishment of political appointees need to be addressed in states, cities, and local districts as a result. It helps put everyone in the system on the same page up and down the various levels. It helps provide better planning, management, supervision, and oversight while setting a foundation for continuity and the bottom line of enhanced instructional performance and increased student achievement. It also excludes distracting political agendas and places consequent focus on the real issues and obstacles that have to be confronted on a daily basis in the pursuit of actually increasing achievement in the most optimal fashion. It also summarily establishes a much-needed structure for oversight connected to systemic issues.

President Joe Biden has taken up the mantle to be the "education president." While in the process of choosing his cabinet, he selected Miguel Cardona from the Connecticut school system as secretary of education on December 23, 2020, as I am writing this piece. This is monumental for a number of reasons: He fits the mold of what is needed on the federal level in line with criteria we just discussed as attributes for the position. He came up from the ranks with proven leadership skills and is open to establishing a "new educational paradigm." Miguel grew up in the public-school system and came from the housing projects of Connecticut. It is a foregone conclusion that not only is he familiar with issues confronted by students in general as well as students from deprived areas, but he also has ideas contemplated and stored over a significant period that he is willing to implement with the aid of contributing stakeholders. A more effaceable system, whose oversight of processes will lead to sustained growth in student achievement and the health and welfare of our children, may reasonably be attained. It may be advantageous to have the term of the secretary of education run so that it does not coincide with the four-year presidential term in order to minimize politics and to maintain educational continuity. It will also be helpful in providing a semblance of a safeguard in the event that future presidents turn out not to have the same regard for the importance of education in our society.

To find a recent example of the impact of politics on educational processes arising out of the leadership level in the federal government, look no further than recent president Trump and the former secretary of education Betsy Devos, his appointee. The president wanted to illegally take funds of 1.5 billion dollars earmarked for public schools in low-income areas under the CARES Act, which would help students get, among other things, laptops for virtual learning as well as funding for programs, materials, and supplies especially needed during the current pandemic situation and give it to private schools, religious schools, and for-profit charter schools. These funds were allotted under Title I funds to public schools. The secretary of education endeavored to follow through with the plan even though it violated the law and was detrimental to students who need it most. A coalition of states organized to sue the federal government and, in particular, the secretary of education over this issue. Political appointees are beholding to whoever appoints them and not to any particular organization, constituency, or system. This must change in education.

States have the auspices in leading the way to more effective educational pursuits. The significance in their funding and placing needed resources on the table, no doubt, guides the thrust of educational reform. However, getting resources and support obviously requires standards to be met in order for funds to be received. The days of throwing money at education and hoping for results are long gone. Here is a case in point regarding the impact of state-level change on institutions under its authority: In response to issues surrounding the police department and the community, New York governor, Mario Cuomo, mandated that all five hundred police departments in New York have meetings with local communities to address how residents wanted the police department to function in their communities. Residents filled out survey questions and shared what they wanted policing to look like in their neighborhoods. Police departments were then to use this feedback to implement needed changes. This process was required in order for state funding to be received. The New York City Council passage of bills as oversight of the police department served to demonstrate how elected officials and government were able to work in a team concept to put into effect essential changes for the community based on what the public desired. It is this format for systemic change that similarly drives our conversation on educational change.

Applicable evaluation tools are always manifested in order for acquiring desired outcomes within organizational systems in general. They continually drive processes that allow implementors to judge whether endeavors are on track to meet expected results. State support from the educational leadership commitment of governors calls for cities to enact procedures that follow through with aspirations and purposes set forth by states. City goals and objectives should be consistent with the states from which they receive funds. However, attributes of various cities do call for adjustments to meet particular unique needs, which require a different set of criteria to be considered for funding purposes. A review of budgets on all levels should reflect the priorities and considerations in question. The federal government ought to be in sync with states on a theme of effective processes, cooperation, support for educational change, and oversight. Too often, it seems that an adversarial relationship is more prevalent than one would ordinarily expect between the levels of federal, state, and city government. Unless we get lucky and get someone on the highest level to see that proposed ideas emanated from needs identified on the service level are carried through, do not expect said needs to be properly addressed as long as politics rule the day. The thought of having a career professional fulfill these roles is, by all means, a sober one that just makes sense. It is obviously a similar situation regarding state educational appointees and city mayoral selections who head education to be on the same page. Political appointees placed on behalf of mayors have simply held the line in too many cases and have been hard-pressed to make impactful change in student achievement over the years. Education in cities and states across the country has amounted to a situation under which unacceptable achievement and high dropout rates have become all too common. This situation is nothing new. We have lived with it and accepted it for years. The perception that continual increase in achievement has made for significant gains has been one that was projected over the last fifty years. When do we get to the point where we can profess that our educational system is effective without reservation?

Positive promotion and publicity of educational processes have far outperformed actual educational production. This is a gap we need to close, and it is a gap only collaboration from the various levels of education can resolve. Corporations, business concerns, and institutions of higher learning have already complained in the past about the quality of students coming out of our schools. It sheds a spotlight on the copious politics connected with the promotion of educational efficacy that has provided a smoke screen to cover up actual failures. It calls for a justification of great discernment and skepticism regarding what is actually taking place. There is no question as to the numbers of well-achieving students produced in spite of systematic conditions, but they amount to less than half of the student population particularly when the dropout rate is factored (See National Center for Education Statistics long-term trends in reading and math and the Nation's Report Card, National Achievement Level Results, or NAEP report).

Schoolwide, districtwide, citywide, and state-wide reporting have indeed been questionable in many cases in the past and remains so to this day. This issue may be open for scrutiny on exactly how processes for reporting are actually carried out and what populations are counted. One consistent factor remains throughout as a constant, and it is that politics drives the narrative.

Currently, the tenure of school superintendents in school districts on average in New York City is close to 3.4 years and 3.8 years nationwide. Educational continuity and leadership that brings sustained achievement to districts cannot be adroitly supported under this type of situation. Superintendents are given three to four years to do a job, and it is simply not working. A three-to-five-year plan may be more advantageous over a span of time—generally considered reasonable to right systematic processes for an institution as expansive as education. Please consider that largely, under present conditions, it will most likely not matter materially how much time superintendents are given to make needed significant growth in student achievement within various school districts. This is due to current circumstances in the system already referred to as "broken." In a healthy organization, time is used to manage developments so that evaluative processes allow for expected growth to equate to projected results. The high superintendent turnover rate makes for a system that hoovers in a constant state of flux. It also suggests loud and clear one of two things: that school districts are not finding adequate leadership to resolve achievement-level issues or that placing good people in a broken system just doesn't work. The good people end up being held accountable for all the ineptitudes a broken system can provide.

The superintendent turnover rate is a function of a system that is in dire straits. Nationwide achievement is below 50 percent, and it has been that way for well over a quarter century. Do you consider half of students achieving a good thing? It is a clear demonstration that we simply are not willing to make the drastic interventions required to get over the quagmire of achievement levels that remain basically unchanged and stagnant for all intents and purposes. Do we really even care enough to make it happen? We do have great people in our system, but the system itself has been broken for a very long time. Implementing partial change in a broken system is like repairing a pipe in a dilapidated building when the system itself is what needs to be changed. The problem is systemic, and our system lags way behind the demands of today's world. When we are capable of addressing this predicament, we will be able to have the luxury of entertaining the perspective of seeing the light at the end of the tunnel. Once systemic issues are addressed, then we will be more able to benefit from addressing programmatic and curriculum inputs, such as looking at things students do outside of school on their own to interest themselves and having a chance to bring them creatively into school curriculums and programs. We will be better prepared to make schools a lab for the extension of student interests and allow for the inculcation of academics in a more creative fashion. We will more effectively have the ability to utilize infomercials, advertisements, and public service announcements similar to what is projected on television or online for products geared toward children, adolescents, young adults, and parents that get them entirely motivated to take action. This includes more research on gaming technologies, which have growth components for various levels as well. It requires an open invitation for imagination and skills, which our young people possess in bulk. Yes, it means bringing their genius to the table along with the professionals and developing ways to accomplishing such processes successfully. Changes in staff characteristics, training, utilization of spaces on and off school sites, and the use of various thematic resources and materials would indelibly become helpful inputs. In short, all of the above will serve to build a better "brand" for education with supporting public relations, marketing, and promotions. These factors influence how education is perceived by the public and thereby facilitate their confidence and support.

Further, in New York City, for example, superintendents give tenure to school principals, and that power is used at their discretion. This may or may not be the best idea for tenure due to the fact that it leaves the matter open to abuse in a system that has already demonstrated what can occur given its political environment and outdated organizational traits.

There are cases of principals who have had tenure withheld for years based on politics and some who have attained tenure in less than two years. Placing people in positions who have proven success in building achievement over time is a legitimate demonstration of criteria for higher responsibility in a system that sorely needs it. Where oversight is needed most, you will find it least on the local level. Behaviors of those on the highest levels of local leadership in education, in many cases, can baffle the mind and be characterized as erratic at best.

We mentioned some of the effects of the short terms superintendents serve and the accompanying politics that take place. A look at the decisions and behaviors that follow as a result has a direct impact on the delivery of education. These behaviors are in no way particular to any one specific local. In New York City during the beginning of the current decade, it was commonplace to find cases of behavior of local leadership to be out of control. Here are actual cases in point: A new superintendent took over a district and put people in place as principals of schools. One principal had no administrative experience on the school level, and another was placed in a school without a proven record of building student achievement. In fact, in the latter case, the superintendent deliberately altered the school performance statistics graphically to show that there was a decline in student performance as a reason for making the personnel change. Ultimately, that principal was eventually caught altering student results on standardized tests and was removed. That same superintendent acquired a position as head of another school system in another state and ended up doing time in prison for taking bribes connected to school programs.

In another case, a school superintendent summarily dismissed four principals and caused another to quit his position. The superintendent's status was in doubt, which gave cause for the removal of any competing considerations for others within the district. Another reason for removal included not getting lunch applications in on time for one principal. The overriding question stands out as to what support was given to aid the situation or whether it was simply an excuse for a "gotcha" moment that fits into a political scheme. In one of the other cases, teachers, parents, students, and community protested a principal's removal, which the school community supported fully. The replacement instituted by the superintendent failed dismally. The same scenario occurred in the third case with the bottom line being that student performance was negatively impacted in each case.

The fourth principal left his position, not wanting to serve under such conditions. A major necessity for educational leaders is to demonstrate the ability to apprise subordinates of their roles, inform them of expectations in fulfilling roles, establish training sessions to provide support for principals to carry out responsibilities, evaluate the effectiveness of implementation, and extend help in problematic areas to assure success. One or more of these responsibilities required more attention in the previous cases. If, on the other hand, all of the above procedures were followed, then it is well within reason to surmise that one does not meet required standards.

Still, in another case, a person actually was unscrupulously placed in a school by a superintendent as an acting principal, not knowing that the superintendent had already selected a person for the position and needed someone to fill it until the person originally selected was released from their school district. The situation would have been incumbent on the leader to explain this at the outset. A monkey wrench was thrown into the process when that principal took the school from the highest number of middle-school incidences in the district to the least number of incidences and from last in attendance to third out of eighteen schools in the district within a span of four months. The superintendent had already made a previous commitment, which led to resorting to finding excuses to remove the acting principal, including getting the other principal sharing the school building to make complaints, and bringing the principal up on fabricated charges. The tactics were unsuccessful, but during these activities, the replacement was made.

That superintendent was made the Deputy Chancellor of education without having any significant or outstanding performance in student achievement in the district! What message does that portray? We all know leadership begins at the top. Who will see to it that commitment and practices vary directly with student achievement? Who will take on the responsibility for the oversight in this educational system?

People can attest to stories like this throughout the system. When the cat is away, the mice will play. Since there is inadequate systematic oversight, especially on the local level, school district leadership behavior sets the tone for a smoke screen that tends to distort the reality of interventions that have to take place for effective student performance to happen.

Additionally, this case in point may seem utterly ridiculous, but during the height of power of the community school boards in New York City, a deputy superintendent sought the favor of a school board president. In his success, as a result, he managed to undermine the existing superintendent and take over as superintendent. He proceeded to put the ousted superintendent in a room to which he reported every day under lock and key. He was isolated from all district office staff, and staff was forbidden to communicate with him.

Personnel searches for educational leaders on the various levels have not affected educational student performance in any significant way for decades. It is why you will always hear emphasis on processes as opposed to product. Changing the system to focus on instilling people not connected to politics and political appointments at the top is, of course, significant. Oversight top to bottom and continuity of goals and objectives make the personnel selection process a more workable solution for bringing in the kind of people who will count.

One of the first responsibilities of personnel administration is fitting people with the task at hand. There are more than enough people in positions who do not fit with tasks to be accomplished. That is a systemic miscue, which must be addressed. Also, to be considered are politics of educational situations where superintendents, fully aware of their short tenure, turn to minimizing the impact of principals in order to secure their positions and cut down options districts may have to attract better leadership. It is always incumbent on leaders to build and encourage leadership and not stifle it. Here is an opportunity to make the system better: by recommending proven and skilled professionals to fill leadership roles in districts having need. It serves to raise the level of effective personnel practices and ultimately facilitates the enhancement of bringing about high student achievement starting from top to bottom.

School Principals

It is common knowledge that oftentimes organizations tend to assume the characteristics of their leaders. It is never more apparent than what you will find in schools. If the principal models the traits he/she wants to see in staff, then it provides a motivation for professional behavior for which staff can aspire. It demonstrates what is expected and establishes a more professional environment. It facilitates the encouragement of processes that aid the realization of desired goals and objectives and provides an example of behavior that can help to expedite a framework for addressing problems and placing everyone on the same page regarding successful completion of tasks. Additionally, it models for students how adults interact as a team of professionals and facilitates the role of students in carrying out their responsibilities as students.

The principal models for staff such things as leadership, professionalism, knowledge, organizational communication, interpersonal relations, teamwork, focus, task orientation, team building, leadership building, work ethic, collegiality, consistency, support for instruction, creativity, and more. These attributes are reflected in staff and serve to permeate the entire organization. This behavior creates a positive and productive school environment and aids in the activities required for enhancing student achievement.

A good and proven practice for principals is to refrain from exhibiting leadership on behalf of minor changes. It allows for others to engage in a quality of leadership that is summarily significant, contagious, and healthy. It's called initiative. Leaving space to have this void filled enables others to be involved in changes and will facilitate the implementation of said changes. It also makes for an environment that inspires others to use their individual strengths to augment overall efforts of the school organization. The principal has only to steer these initiatives in a direction that matches people appropriately with the task and makes it possible for staff to, as some of my folk would say, "git in where they fit in." It also encourages staff differentiation, self-actualization, and a robust organization. It makes for good energy in the school and, along with student programs, supports an exciting environment for learning.

This type of activity calls for an understanding of people (people skills) and interpersonal relations in having the wisdom and knowledge to motivate and significantly allow for growth development and leadership of school members. It also provides a template for teachers as they help students grow and take an active part in their learning.

Schools are community institutions, and principals are community leaders. This notion has been a historical and traditional acceptance through the years. Once schools began to be filled with staff from various other areas, the concept of community went out the window, so to speak. This is a hypothesis that needs to be adequately addressed in education. Principals, as community leaders, would visit churches and other community organizations, speak on behalf of the school, and facilitate community outreach. What effect do you think this would have on parent cooperation and participation, student behavior, community agencies with guidance counselors, school events, and school/community programs? Principals should not be locked into the school building all day. Additionally, putting in eleven and twelve hours a day (as some principals have been known to do) does not equate to higher student achievement. It relates more to the law of diminishing utility (which states that once you reach the most optimal level of productivity, there is a limit to how much more you will benefit) than it does to the goal of enhanced student performance. It also demonstrates the need for better planning and use of staff, which is a formula for efficiency. If someone is not doing their job, provide them all the help for which they are entitled but refrain from allowing stress to come your way as a result. If you happen to be functioning in an environment of stress, understand that it goes down the organization and not upward, with each staff member responsible for their own job. Everyone has to be held accountable to the role for which they signed up. Principals have to demonstrate the healthy and enriched life they want for their students, staff, and community and, in effect, have a life.

Assistant Principals

For all practical intents and purposes, the assistant principal runs the school. He/she is charged with carrying out the operational aspects of implementing school programs, providing program planning and evaluation, supervising staff, training teachers, setting schedules, interacting with parents and students, coordinating processes regarding student behavior, and facilitating quality classroom instruction. The APs are the glue that bring together harmonious interactions between and among the various staff members, parents, and students. APs report to the principal as needed but must have a set time to meet daily to discuss progress of the operation. Unless there is a teacher trainer on staff, the AP generally trains teachers. Obviously, with their various multiple duties, there is just not enough time to train teachers appropriately. Even teacher trainers have their own schedule and are not capable of devoting the time needed in many cases. This is serious! Training teachers is our frontline attack on implementing the delivery and quality of instruction. This area can procure great rewards with more suitable attention. It cannot be stated enough how rearranging funding priorities to provide more appropriate staffing for professional development of teachers in particular and educational staffing in general would impact society by providing an upgrade to the quality of the workforce. This would affect every other aspect of our culture. Let us recall and remind ourselves of the power of what education can do. It's why we continue to advocate raising teacher salaries but not blindly. Raising salaries does not equate to increased production or achievement. In a broken system, it almost does not matter what you do as far as resolutions unless the system is fixed.

Teachers and Students

To teach does not necessarily mean that one is learning. It demonstrates that one is clarifying, explaining, and communicating. The antonym to teaching is learning, which is to absorb, understand, or discover. You have probably witnessed much teaching, but how much learning was actually taking place? Performance test results indicate that less than half of all students are learning (National Center for Education Statistics). Are performance test results a legitimate indicator of what students actually learn? Some would reply, apparently, yes. Colleges, corporations, business concerns, and employers in general complain about the student product they are getting. That is why colleges and universities have developed programs to help students get up to speed upon entry rather than lose their student population.

Significantly, college enrollment has been experiencing a pattern of decline in recent years. The present pandemic has played a role in greatly decreasing college enrollment, as students and parents are fearful of the increased spread of the coronavirus we have witnessed on multiple college campuses. It has however, had a positive effect on local community college enrollment as a result, due to the fact that students are able to commute back and forth to school or study virtually from home nearby. Businesses, corporations, federal, state and local government, organizations and individuals have the ability to address this need with grants, scholarships, fellowships, apprenticeships and tuition donations that will ultimately benefit every segment of our society. More of our focus is required to invite the above entities to execute the educational propulsion we deserve.

It should be understood, as in any profession, that what teachers bring to the table regarding instructional efficacy varies with the plethora of knowledge, understanding, and experience in their background and the level of motivation they inspire in the classroom setting. A teacher who typically deals with school-age children in his/her family will have an understanding of children that is different from someone who has very little interaction with school-age students in their own life. Interfacing with school-age people is an advantage. It feeds into helping to know what makes them tick while lowering the generation gap and improving their taste and thirst for learning.

A teacher who is a more informed person in his/her own right will generally have more resources to call upon to add to the mix of classroom activities. Similarly, teachers having special talents in which to engage outside of the profession, such as artists, athletes, tailors, musicians, chess players, all possess characteristics that can serve to motivate students regardless of their scholastic area of study. Creatively, teachers, teacher trainers, supervisors, and students can engage in collaborations that present the optimal set of outcomes for successful implementation of approaches. Such attributes make a difference in creating a learning environment that is interesting, flexible, and open to the absorption of concepts and ideas.

School Counselors

The roles of school personnel have changed in substantial ways due to the current COVID-19 pandemic. The enhanced duress it has placed on school counselors only serves to add to the stressful environment surrounding school activities. Students coming from areas that are disadvantaged, rural or homeless, face challenges connected with insecure family income, living conditions, and food situations. How will they be able to survive before we can even begin to entertain the idea of achieving in school? How will they be able to acquire the necessary support for learning under virtual education guidelines? What type of support will be effective for parents to help guide their child's learning? The answer to these questions calls for more systemic focus and a priority that centers on fundamental planning before throwing our children into the lion's den. Some places, like New York, at one point, boasted a school spread rate at 0.6 percent, which was a very low spread rate compared to many schools across the country. However, can we afford to accept any level of spread rate statistics in our schools? During the second wave of COVID-19 spread across the country, the New York rate increased to double digits, which signaled the beginning of the greatest spread of disease in American history.

Additionally, the same insecurities have affected the lives of working-class and middle-class families who have become subjected to layoffs due to the impact of the COVID-19 pandemic on businesses and the economy. It was estimated by the national food bank (feedingamerica.org) that one in five adults were food insecure and one in four children were as well. Students bring stressful home environments to school whether it is via distant learning or in-school classrooms, which may be characterized by various types of behavior. Absenteeism, unfocused attention, acting out, disinterest, and sickness are some of the traits exhibited. School counselors and teachers are, many times, the first-line in identifying these symptoms. Families may need to be directed to agencies and services that can help address such problems that involve local food banks, unemployment offices, and various services to children and families.

It was mentioned by New York City's first lady, Chirlane McCrae (who is chair of the Mayor's Fund to Advance New York City and the driving force of ThriveNYC in which she extensively helped to improve mental-health and substance-abuse services), that we are void of an effective and functional system for addressing mental-health services in America. Mayor de Blasio consequently made it a priority to then add services to schools that would center on more social emotional support for trauma services and universal screening for students' mental health care. He pointed out that coordinated efforts in mental health care across the country are simply nonexistent. This effort lies at the forefront of what schools need to support the education of children. It is particularly relevant to the current environment and is yet another factor of systematic maladies exposed by the influence of the coronavirus pandemic. Take for example the situation surrounding the recent insurrection and siege of the United States Capitol building by homegrown terrorists; how will parents explain this occurrence to their children? What effect will it have on democracy and the worldview of young adults who study American history? How will the stress experienced by adults affect family dynamics in an environment of pandemic disease, unemployment, racial unrest, and insurrection? What impression will it have on children in households, and how will it influence their student school performance? Environmental predicaments such as these imply that if you want an increase in student achievement, it will behoove you to invest in support for student learning by focusing on enhancing the remedy for psychological impediments that can serve to prevent the brilliance of students from taking place.

Parents and teacher aides with children during hybrid learning also play an important role in identifying student behaviors and providing intervention in helping students remain on point. These issues require an expanded role on the part of guidance counselors, which is why I recommend they have either an assistant to follow up with students experiencing the abovementioned insecurities or someone whose capacity is to monitor these processes and function with resource agencies to provide assistance to families. We can also note that it has never been more apparent than during this time that school districts, special-education supervisors, and teachers will need to arrive at an effective plan for providing applicable practices for students at home formerly requiring aides to enable support for distant learning.

CHAPTER 8

Student Growth

How is it possible for a student to reach grade 8 with a fourth- or fifth-grade reading level? It takes place more often than I care to mention. Putting meaningful accountability and intervention measures in place to address this situation and similar instances of low achievement is obviously the answer. Well, why isn't it done? I have seen instances whereby a student is left back more than once before grade 8. What is wrong with that picture? It's the same over-riding theme that has characterized systematic efforts toward realizing goals of reaching and sustaining high achievement. It is a theme devoid of necessary commitments to accountability and intervention. It is a theme whose commitment must be shared from the very top and followed through to the lowest levels of the delivery chain. That is why more involvement and commitment is absolutely essential from the national level to the state, city, and local community district levels. Basically, what the past half century has demonstrated is that if the country's top executive is not on board, then you can be assured that the achievement level of students will not be attainable to reach even the 50th percentile nationally on grade reading levels. If there is nobody home at the top, generally speaking, it then becomes infinitely more futile to implement sustained growth in the various levels throughout the system. Obviously, there may be pockets of exceptions which need to be studied and replicated.

We have witnessed recently what takes place when there is a lack of leadership at the very top during the current pandemic crisis. It added up to national systematic malfunction and outcomes that exposed a failure to act. Outcomes of education have demonstrated that it has been in a crisis mode for years. Our young people are looking for answers. Their frustration with today's institutions has brought institutions under attack precisely because they have professed to be about efficacy, but their processes dictate otherwise. Young people say, "Enough is Enough." It may be too early to surmise the current drop out rate for 2021. You can probably bet that is has been negatively impacted by the Corona Virus pandemic.

In special education, there are IEPs (individual-ized education plans) that give a plan for a particu-lar student's special educational needs. The students are evaluated, placed in a class that is designed to address the educational requirement of the student, and assessed along the way to see to what extent the service is aiding student progress. Well, in reality, there have been all kinds of problems with this pic-ture especially because some evaluated students were oftentimes placed in classes with the wrong services and left there without a proper placement for signif-icant periods of time. This situation can take place over a number of years. I have witnessed cases of some evaluations happen without ever placing students. Cases of this nature were frequently noted when it was found that some students exhibiting acting-out behavior in general-education classes were supposed to be placed in special education (not to imply that acting out behavior is synonymous with being a spe-cial education student). Additionally, much of the ongoing evaluations required by IEPs were either too infrequent or not followed up appropriately, result-ing in situations where students were left in classes with incorrect services or inadequate services.

Intervention measures that allow for correc-tions to take place in the IEP have to be assessed as to whether the plan is working or not. Amazingly, I found these issues to be prevalent years ago in my capacity as a Districtwide Special Education Placement Officer, and the same issues are still evident to this day. I recently viewed an individual education plan for the nephew of a friend and found that he was given services that were from a grade 2 evaluation. By grade 3, he completely overcame to the point where his diction and speech were very good (speech therapy). Yet it remained on his IEP year after year to grade 5. His actual area of special-education need was identified without follow-up as to whether or not he was actually receiving the service. If you are in touch with educators, you will find frequent stories of this nature.

Also, funds earmarked for special education need to be restricted for that program and not for general education. In recent interviews with educators, it became apparent that this was an issue that takes place more than we may care to think. It again points out the fact that oversight may be the single most important factor under leadership that should absorb our attention as we attempt to create "a new educational paradigm," one that works for us all and particularly for our students.

There is a window for which teachers are most effective during their careers in both programs (general and special education). There needs to be something in place for teachers who have spent twenty years or more in the classroom to transition correctly out of the classroom, whether it be for retirement, quasi retirement, or an intermediate position before retirement, to prevent the crude situation of forcing them out in favor of paying less for beginning teachers or for productivity issues. Oversight to address these issues properly is essential.

CHAPTER 9

Community

A dditionally, note that current issues regarding community empowerment reveal relevant conversations surrounding those vested in the community. Most teachers servicing communities of color live elsewhere. It takes what has historically been an essential part of the community out of the equation. How does that affect service and achievement? What are the perspectives and attitudes of those outside of the community, and how do they view the students, parents, and community institutions of which they are part? This is a current-day issue that has been brought to light over the years as a result of actions of other community organizations such as the police department. It is an issue that requires more exploration in order to find an effective solution.

Certainly, community agencies and organizations are established to reflect the needs, interests, and well-being of its residents. Apparently, activity antithetical to the health, safety, and security of community residents cannot exist within the realm of acceptable measures or definitions of what the concept of "community" dictates. It is well within reason to reject such activity as a nonproductive by-product that represents a stray from what communities require in order to attain the most basic foundations of life, liberty, and the pursuit of happiness. Issues such as this speak to the condition of many school-age students who must endeavor to succeed and get an education in spite of poor living conditions, poor health services, food deprivation, social and environmental threats, family situations, and poverty. These are factors relevant to communities in city schools and many rural areas as well. The COVID-19 pandemic of 2020 has not only exacerbated these factors but also facilitated focus on the very issues that have haunted Americans for centuries. It places profound emphasis on doing something about it now or forever hold your peace. The future of our children depends on the extent to which we address these inequities.

CHAPTER 10

Considerations on School Openings

The COVID-19 pandemic led to vigorous discussion as to when and how schools would reopen. A nationwide plan for this situation had not been forthcoming thereby leaving individual states to arrive at their own solutions. This could only serve to exacerbate the current problematic differences in the quality of education in each state throughout the country as the coronavirus continually forced school closings. It impacted the funding curve for states and discounted the particular needs of low-income areas. It called for increased funding and adept leadership to address the pandemic impact on education nationally. Instead, we endured political solutions on the national level that amounted to a perspective of shortsightedness and neglect when systemic solutions that brought fundamental and lasting change were obviously the order of the day.

Decisions to reopen schools will more than likely take place before the release of this writing, but I will mention a few (of which there are many) considerations that matter on the local level. Lest we forget, schooling in general has, by and large, always been composed of group activity (i.e., classes, group counseling, morning lineup, auditorium, physical education, student government, cafeteria time, school clubs, teams, busing, and more). Couple these situations with basic school trafficking entering and exiting the building. Schools have right and left side hall movement and up and downside staircases. There are many schools where this procedure is not strictly followed. It has always been a safety issue. We can see that, now more than ever, safety guidelines need to be upheld. Consider also students having underlying conditions and the plan for their well-being. Busing routes will also need to be refigured, as some parents may opt out with their children in favor of virtual learning and school schedules for hybrid learning (in-school classroom versus remote learning). This will indubitably dictate changes in bus routing.

Additionally, yet to be ultimately determined are the following questions: How will periodic testing for students and staff take place? How often will disinfecting and cleaning be accomplished? How will

PPE materials and supplies be managed? What procedures will be put in place for those testing positive? How will the rate of community transmission affect the school environment? What alternative plans have been put in place for the various outcomes? How will outreach for parents be sculptured to align with the new situation? Keep in mind that "impact of COVID-19, aside from apparent mortalities, can also include long-term injury to lungs, heart, vascular system, neurological deficits, and cognitive deficits that can plague victims even years after vaccines will be implemented" as per Dr. Peter Hotez, Director of Texas Children's Hospital Center for Vaccine Development. Couple this information with the fact that incidences and deaths from COVID-19 were up to three times as high in neighborhoods of Black and Brown people. During the flu season, we experienced the most devastating pandemic of our time. How are we to overcome the effects of this? Newly developed vaccines were not projected to be distributed to the general public until spring of 2021. There is much food for thought here Federal, state, city, and local school districts are inevitably required to collaborate within a team concept to arrive at solutions. Having vested parties on the same page will certainly go a long way toward increasing chances of finding success in controlling the spread and incidence of the coronavirus.

Note that students under ten years old were the least tested for COVID-19, and to this point, there has been limited data for this population. More information is vital for testing, tracing, and tracking this group in particular. In an announcement regarding school reopening during the second wave of the pandemic, Governor Cuomo of New York stated that 20 percent of students would receive testing every two weeks from grades pre-K to 5K during December of 2020. This amounted to the first such situation in the country. More and more, we saw that the COVID-19 virus was traveling from young people to older, more at-risk people. Roughly one-third of teachers in education are over fifty years of age nationwide. This is the most at-risk population. Similar to how teachers often catch colds from their students is also how the virus can be contracted. Remember, it only takes one student or adult to test positive, then everyone to whom that person was in contact must be quarantined for fourteen days. After which time, they must be retested. Since newly discovered vaccines are already in the distribution phase, it is not entirely clear how long they will prevent the disease or whether vaccines can prevent the same people from getting the virus again once they return to the same environment over a period of time. The jury is still out on whether this can happen. Answers regarding the vaccines have arrived almost each day since new developments have taken place at every turn. It must be stated in advance that these questions may be moot points once more information is amassed.

It is our hope that succeeding chapters will serve to illuminate concepts and ideas visited in this discussion. More than enough responsibility is placed on educators to perform in a vacuum that is replete with traps, uncertainty, and life-threatening dangers connected with the COVID-19 environment. There are no assurances that teachers will not be exposed to the virus and its communicable properties; therefore, they are obligated to take control of what decision-making alternatives are within the scope of their arena. Teacher unions have made inroads in fulfilling some of these issues. Obstacles and problems will need to be continually addressed due to the fact that necessary changes are still taking place as more information is gathered concerning the coronavirus.

CHAPTER 11

Professional Development

The following ideas are prefaced by mandates of the current COVID-19 environment and the restrictions it requires. It is suggested that, wherever possible, virtual distance activities be incorporated to align with professional development processes. Additionally, it is worthwhile to mention that these ideas are in no way anything new. The institution of these processes needs to demonstrate a direct relationship to their contribution to achievement. Educators have taken part in some of the greatest professional-development sessions. What impact did the assemblies have on building an upward curve year after year on achievement? Most national achievement levels hoover within a particular range below the 50th percentile (the Nation's Report Card, National Achievement Level Results, National Assessment of Educational Progress [NAEP]). The fact that less than half the students in the nation can read or do math on a proficient level is mind-boggling! How do we break that plain and go beyond the 50th percentile in reading and math? Goals are set for a reason. Significantly, they are ends for which to aspire. However, the roads traveled to reach such destinations call for focus as to more efficacy in directly relating to heightened achievement.

The following acronym "COWBIRDS", is derived from supervisory sessions I have attended in the past that relates to a generic formula for instituting professional development. I have updated each section to incorporate my own perspective.

C—Conferences, Community, Staff Meetings

Preparing teachers to perform is a vital obligation that requires more consideration than we have been willing to affect. Teachers, for the most part, need to be guided more effectively into the roles necessary to deliver appropriate levels of instruction essential for today's students. Everything that is done in this endeavor should be evaluated on the level of the extent of student progress and achievement. It seems the success of professional development is inordinately placed on processes without a direct relationship to student achievement outcomes. This gap must be closed in order to acquire the desired student results. The previous chapter outlined some specific activities regarding professional development for new teachers. Many of the same elements apply here as well. These efforts may be aggregated by establishing conferences and staff meetings centered on facilitating the ability of teachers to close the gap between what is taught and the level of resultant student achievement. Unleash the experts, technology, and tools to turn the theory into reality.

What teachers actually cover in the classroom and what students are expected to learn is the gap to which I refer. We seem to take for granted that curriculum concepts are covered and test students on what we feel they should have learned. What is left out of this picture is the extent to which mastery of the content was actually learned. Obviously, it is incumbent upon us to do better in ascertaining that students know said curriculum before statewide or citywide tests are administered so that we can get a suitable understanding or projection of the outcome. Judging from the outcome of national achievement testing data, it is evident that what students are learning in school is not the same as what testing data shows (google NAEP data referred to previously). Much of the content on national and statewide data just does not simulate what is going on in the classrooms. What is actually taught and what students actually learn would do well to be monitored more directly. For example, if the concept of the three forms of matter was being taught in grade 7 science, application drills or exercises following the lesson should show the extent of how many students were successful in understanding the concepts. Results should be documented. Follow-up homework would further provide an opportunity for students whose understanding may be in question. The review of homework and the teacher's response to questions on homework the next day are totally important! This cannot be stressed enough. Here is where clarification matters for students who may need more attention: The number of remaining students who become successful as a result of such clarifications would do well to also be documented. "Do Now" problems (or reasonable facsimiles thereof) are brief exercises often utilized in the classroom by teachers to further expand on previous concepts given in order to engage students the moment they enter the classroom, during individualization of homework review, or while attendance is done. It may also serve as another opportunity to clarify previous concepts or provoke thought for what is to be learned that day. Students who have new learning as a result of this process should also be documented with results to be inserted into their IEP (Individual Education Plan).

In addition, weekly quizzes and monthly tests offer another prospect for evaluating the extent of student understanding and giving a clearer picture of the projection of student achievement. Results should be documented for each student. The record will then show what was actually taught and what was truly learned. It will demonstrate what actual learning in the classroom is taking place and what districtwide, statewide, and nationwide testing should cover. If there are concept mandates on the various levels, then accurate testing instruments and oversight should be put in place to actually monitor classroom-learning documentation and the volume and rate of how much content is evidently covered. Some teachers are able to cover content at greater rates and volume. Note that this process calls for new testing grids to be developed that take into consideration the volume of curricula covered per class, learning rates per class and student mastery documentation. It requires that state, city and local school-districts work in unison to develop a formula and management tools. Students cannot be faulted or short-changed on achievement levels due to assumptions of what they were supposed to learn. This is why the proposed evaluative documentation is suggested. It gives teachers, students, parents, and supervisors a more accurate account of student progress. It also gives test administrators information on what they should actually test. Setting proficiency levels has little value when there are so many inconsistencies and variations on what actually takes place in the classroom and with the characteristics of teachers that are so different. Please note that these processes will not work in a broken system. Suggestions made previously regarding various level oversight and support will be required. These are themes that would do well to surface during conferences and staff meetings to impact curriculum.

O—Observations

What teachers learn from being observed by supervisors or teacher trainers while delivering instruction is invaluable. Teachers need guidance on the processes of observations so that they are not viewed as "gotcha" moments. Supervisors require more appropriate training so that this process is instituted successfully. Education teaches us that growth continues throughout life, and it is certainly no different in a professional environment. Growth is one of the keys to life. It makes us all better. We are happier and better for growing, and it enhances everyone within our midst. There is both an art and science to helping adults to grow. Chief among attributes needed for one's success in this undertaking are people skills, knowledge, understanding, and motivational and inspirational approaches.

This may or may not be relevant, but I used to sell *Colliers Encyclopedias*. It called for knocking on people's doors, gaining acceptance and entrance, and making a pitch for something that may have been the last thing on their minds. What got them to open the door was my appearance. What motivated them to invite me in was my approach and personality. What got them to buy something they were not even thinking about was my knowledge of the product and its attributes to benefit them. The point here is to show things that matter to people when interacting. We are all aware of this to some degree. Employing these things may not matter much, but not employing them could mean incalculable chances for teacher-growth opportunities and quality instruction that facilitates learning achievement.

Observations should be positive, nurturing, informative, open, and transparent. They should be encouraging and developmental in nature. They should be supportive and allow for the learning modality of individuals. This provides a path for teachers to transfer what they learn into teaching approaches with students whenever possible. The same skills required for teachers to teach students also apply to adults with some variation. Importantly, schools need to have the option of outside resource people to get this right.

W—Workshops

Workshops with teachers allow for hands-on undertakings. They provide for modeling behaviors and procedures for interacting with students and experimenting with various methods of delivery, instructional approaches, questioning techniques, and modes of creative processes. They also provide a vehicle for generating best practices intended for particular sets of students. The workshop is a great setup for meeting particular teacher areas of concern and should, no doubt, be implemented more often. Workshops are relevant to all aspects of education, including organizational, administrative, and supervisory activities. They serve to foster smooth organizational processes, effective and efficient administrative accomplishments, and laudable supervisory practices. They also serve to enhance the flexibility of educational pursuits through expansion of the knowledge base.

B—Bulletins, Buddy System

The buddy system enables teachers to work together under a team concept to enhance each other's ability to implement teaching processes while providing collegial support and comradery. This helps build a stable teaching core and a healthy environment for working and coping together. Handbooks and bulletins provide online guidelines for various methodologies that teachers or administrators may consult at any particular moment via iPad, laptop, Apple watch, desktop, or a combination of a multitude of the latest technologies.

I—Intervisitations, Informal Observations

Teachers having an occasion to see others in action is an invaluable experience. They would have an opportunity to see their buddies teach as well as exemplary teachers engaging in instructional delivery. This enables them to learn from one another. Feedback they share can be only among them or set up to have supervisory feedback, for example, in the case of viewing exemplary lesson deliveries. Additionally, there is much to be gained from setting up informal visits with supervisors to gain added feedback on sculpturing lessons and lesson delivery while building quality student interaction.

R—Recommended Readings, Research

Research and additional readings add to the resources teachers bring to the table. To be informed and to research ideas only serve to heighten their ability to bring excitement and new information to lessons for students. It also models for students how study and research can make what they learn more interesting. Online searches provide vivid and expansive learning situations, which students may already be aware. The use of laptops and school computers in the classroom or in distance learning can underscore this activity.

D—Demonstration Lessons, Exhibits, Displays

Demonstration lessons provide an example to teachers on how to deliver instruction. They are generally given by master teachers who have particular expertise in certain areas. This practice can be used for new teachers and inexperienced teachers as well as veteran teachers. It is a great activity for those entering teaching from other careers. It can also be used to introduce new areas of curriculum as well as use of the latest technology.

Exhibits and displays highlight materials and resources that may be used to bring more interest and attention to a wide range of topics connected with instructional efficacy.

S—Supervisors, Superintendents, Students, Self-Evaluation

It is up to supervisors to oversee pulling the title wave of instruction together. Their work with teacher trainers and teachers provides the backbone of what teaching will look like in a school. They will need to be ever mindful that the gist of their contributions has to relate ultimately and directly to growth in student achievement levels. This is a natural outcome when all stakeholders are on the same page. Stakeholders include levels of federal, state, city, and local representatives along with school staff, community, parents, and students.

Obviously, leadership is a central factor in making appropriate education happen. It is tantamount on every level and within levels. It sets direction and ensures that educational goals and objectives are realized. School superintendents function more on policy and policy decision-making than do leaders in subordinate levels who must focus more on operational processes. It is why the team concept of educational pursuits requires every segment to function on the same page as opposed to existing as separate entities. This is significant because it affects oversight, particularly, as well as continuity of service in administration and supervision, instructional practices, and ultimately, student achievement.

Policies and decisions implemented on the district superintendent level call for an alignment with the aforementioned factors so that there is an effective remedy for hitches in the delivery of services that are recognized through oversight processes. However, these obstacles cannot be met appropriately if support from sectors, such as city-, state-, and federal-level education policy decision-makers, are not working in a team concept and on the same page as those in descending levels. Leadership from the very top matters. The lack of it renders great leadership activity down through the system akin to placing a thumb in the hole of a dam. The nonexistence of appropriate leadership can influence the bottom line of an entire system to the point of stagnation that ultimately prevents systematic growth and the ability to incorporate ideas that serve to make the institution of education work successfully for all.

Students bear the brunt of whatever is ailing in the system. The fact that less than half of our students are achieving affects the quality and effectiveness of the functioning of our society. There should be no small wonder as to the existence of the myriad of societal issues we are confronted with today. Less than half of those emanating from the educational system do not know the country's history or possess adequate knowledge of science, math, or reading (google national educational achievement). Even some of the achievement statistics can be suspect because those reporting statistics are sometimes skewed or simply inaccurate. Let's face it. No school or school district wants to be viewed as being incompetent. There are those of us who have firsthand knowledge of such unspoken situations and, with the least bit of investigation, you will find stories abound; enough said.

Self-evaluation is something that must take place within the realm of all positive outcomes. Focus on growth, and everything else will follow. This comment attempts to provide a backdrop for how the individual fits in with professional development from within the confines of their own personal perspective. It is a retrospective view that has its roots in the specter of continual improvement for the sake of giving better service. It is no more or no less than the healthy activity in which we engage throughout life. It is connected with being the best version of one's self. It is a function of what education teaches and a necessary feature particularly for enlivening stagnancy, thought provocation, and creativity. It is also an activity in which individuals and organizations need to indulge in order to assume appropriate perspectives on the big picture and their roles in bringing objectives to fruition. It is a healthy process and not a challenge. The former factors relate to an inquisitive search for optimal practices in order to give better service to others, and the latter relates to competition with one's self or others in an environment associated with a more stressful atmosphere.

CHAPTER 12

Administrators

Many years ago, the Department of Education in New York City provided professional licenses for administrators and supervisors. These licenses were appropriated in various areas of curriculum—supervision, administration, and policy decision-making. They included levels such as superintendent, deputy superintendent, principal, assistant principal, and central and district office educational administrators. Prospective applicants for positions were required to take a test in order to acquire licenses for consideration of administrative positions. If they were chosen through an interview process, then they were placed accordingly. Some examples of license titles included educator administrator, senior subject area instructional program management specialist, senior curriculum development and coordination instructional specialist, and senior staff development and training instructional specialist, with multiple administrative area licenses and certifications.

There was an abundance of administrative and supervisory training sessions established for prospective administrators during the unique time period of the eighties in New York City, which helped to make those consuming courses particularly astute as they endeavored to take on new administrative and supervisory roles. The sessions were established by administrators in the field who had particular expertise and experience and were designed to prepare participants to test successfully for the various Department of Education licenses and certifications. Information received during sessions was not of the sort one would accrue through theory in graduate study, but rather, it was actually aligned directly to on-the-job practices. Sessions were not connected to the central board of education. They were established under the auspices of individuals and organizations.

Some of the types of administrative courses included the Wilson Consultant Corporation Supervisory Preparatory Course, which was headed by Mr. C. Wilson and Dr. Gladstone Atwell (middle School 61 in Crown Heights Brooklyn, New York, is named after him). It covered the various aspects of supervision and administration. One of the first things they discussed was something you rarely hear about these days. They state the following information was derived from Curriculum Bulletin No. 1, 1955–56 Series curriculum development in the elementary schools board of education of the city of New York. Aims and objectives of public education in New York City were as follows:

1. *Character.* To develop the basis for rich, useful, moral, and ethical living in a society promoting the common welfare
2. *Health.* To develop and maintain a sound body and to establish wholesome mental and emotional attitudes and habits
3. *Exploration.* To discover, develop, and direct individual interests, attitudes, and habits
4. *Expression and appreciation.* To develop an appreciation and enjoyment of beauty and to develop powers of creative expression
5. *Social relationships.* To develop desirable social attitudes and relationships within the family, the school, and the community
6. *Critical and sound thinking.* To stimulate the inquiring mind and sound thinking functionally necessary for the development

of reasoning based on adequate hypotheses
supported by facts and principles

7. *American heritage*. To develop pride and
faith in American democracy and respect
for the dignity and worth of individuals
and people, regardless of race, religion,
nationality, or socioeconomic status

8. *Knowledge and skills*. To develop command,
in accordance with ability, of the common
integrating habits, learning, and skills

9. *Economic relationships*. To develop an
awareness and appreciation of economic
processes and of all who serve in the world

10. *Sciences*. To build interest and appreciation
for science and technology

There was also the Paul Treatment course, the Dr.
Tom Monteiro course, the Sasserath-Gerchick coach-
ing course, the Education Supervisor Preparatory
Course (my course), and others too numerous to
mention here.

Similarly, there were enough courses to attract
and entice a healthy market for administrative professional development. This is sort of a short historical list of educational professionals and experts
who laid a foundation for shouldering administrative

and supervisory practices dedicated to meeting the needs of those in the business of education who were searching for more preparation in order to endeavor to run schools and school districts with better efficacy. Obviously, it is still a work in progress after all these years.

The Department of Education no longer utilizes the above titles, rendering the need for such specializations unwarranted from their perspective. Consequently, the pool of such specialists began to become slimmer as time moved forward, and the results to the system became evident in the decreasing amount of highly skilled and knowledgeable administrators who were born of the baby boomer generation. The system was left with a huge experience gap. It amounted to the first large wave of experienced administrators leaving the system for retirement from 2000 to 2010 when early retirement packages were set into motion due to the economy and the city budget crisis. The immediate impact was that replacements tended to be younger and inexperienced and were left without appropriate training and mentorship. In a number of cases, much of the tutelage and training for school principals was taken on by the Department of Education who, in turn, made an attempt to use retired principals to fulfill the training gap. The program suffered from a lack of real commitment and lack of appropriate resources and from some staff who were simply not up to the task. Criteria for selecting mentors left much to be desired. The bottom line of negligible increased systematic student performance exposed the program to much scrutiny.

School principals will tell you to this very day about the level and extent of interaction and direction they receive from central board and how much of it is questionable, particularly when directives are emanated from those with little or no school experience. It must be noted that this situation (as do most systemwide operations) requires a macro perspective of the entire system in order to make a more definitive analysis. Oversight, policy decisions, and operational standards need to be derived from the very top of the chain and be consistent throughout in order to provoke real change at the service level.

CHAPTER 13

Conclusions

The production function of education amounts to all the inputs from the various levels of responsibility, including federal, state, city, local district, schools, parents, students, and community. Support for instruction is everyone's concern. The extent to which a cohesive plan is developed for consistent educational processes and procedures throughout the system, will dictate the degree of quality achievement experienced by our students on the service level. Who will coordinate these efforts and who will monitor oversight activities will depend on the type of collaboration established by states and the federal government. Education in America is delivered through the auspices of states. It is suggested that the secretary of education coordinate with states so that there is a consistent plan for oversight throughout the system as well as mutual understanding of goals and objectives to enable each state to have the same quality and level of support. This helps prevents states from having different standards and processes that make for inordinate or less than appropriate educational growth toward increased achievement levels.

When over seventy million people voted for someone to be president of the United States who demonstrated no respect for values, rule of law, empathy and cohesion amongst American people; we reached the point where how people are educated in society matters. The notion of good character in leaders was generally implied and taken for granted until we witnessed the experience of a leader without it. It makes a difference when one has historical perspective regarding mistakes of the past that call for correction in the future. It, of course, matters for our children and consequent generations: that to be the best they can be is associated with what they can contribute to the general good and how one's own preparation, skills, and knowledge can serve to make life better for everyone in society. That is what education is supposed to do. Your successes become everyone's success. Ideals are essential because they give us a reason to strive and become better. In the midst of our current quagmire, there is a golden opportunity to restack the foundational building blocks that have set the basis for an educational system to thrive and inject a new energy into its purpose. Go forth and be great.

About the Author

E ric Frazier's background in the field of education encompasses the gamut of what an educational professional could experience in a career. He taught on levels from preschool to college. He trained one-third of the school district/central board test coordinator liaisons in New York City under Director Ron Ladonne. He was the head of testing for all students including preschoolers in the areas of cognitive ability, hearing, and kinetic aptitude in the Brooklyn, New York, school districts of East New York, Brownsville, (District 23) and Bedford-Stuyvesant (District 16) and school-based testing in Crown Heights, Brooklyn (District 17). He worked in every New York City school district between his capacities as a central board of education school improvement facilitator and central board school district test liaison, interfacing with hundreds of schools. He was among the first to teach special-education students in Bedford-Stuyvesant. He was a master teacher who produced master teachers in his role as a teacher trainer and supervisor. He held such school-based positions as pupil personnel coordinator, dean, teacher trainer, career education instructor, and chairman of the discipline and school safety committees. Additionally, on the junior high school level, he taught reading, writing, science, including biology, chemistry, ecology, physics, and social studies, Black American history, public speaking, and career education. On the high-school level, he taught Black American history after school, and on the college level, he taught as an assistant at Southern Illinois University. He was a sensitivity group instructor and teaching assistant in the Black American Studies Program as well as the first university graduate in that area of study. He published a manual entitled *Writing*, which was sponsored through the auspices of School District 23 in Brooklyn, New York. Each New York City school district was invited to implement it into their instructional programs. Consequently, Eric was commissioned to develop a writing curriculum for the city of New York by then Chancellor of Education Anthony Alvarado. His school-based administration and supervision experience took place in the form of principal (middle school and elementary school), assistant principal (elementary and middle school),

About the Author

E ric Frazier's background in the field of education encompasses the gamut of what an educational professional could experience in a career. He taught on levels from preschool to college. He trained one-third of the school district/central board test coordinator liaisons in New York City under Director Ron Ladonne. He was the head of testing for all students including preschoolers in the areas of cognitive ability, hearing, and kinetic aptitude in the Brooklyn, New York, school districts of East New York, Brownsville, (District 23) and Bedford-Stuyvesant (District 16) and school-based testing in Crown Heights, Brooklyn (District 17). He worked in every New York City school district between his capacities as a central board of education school improvement facilitator and central board school district test liaison, interfacing with hundreds of schools. He was among the first to teach special-education students in Bedford-Stuyvesant. He was a master teacher who produced master teachers in his role as a teacher trainer and supervisor. He held such school-based positions as pupil personnel coordinator, dean, teacher trainer, career education instructor, and chairman of the discipline and school safety committees. Additionally, on the junior high school level, he taught reading, writing, science, including biology, chemistry, ecology, physics, and social studies, Black American history, public speaking, and career education. On the high-school level, he taught Black American history after school, and on the college level, he taught as an assistant at Southern Illinois University. He was a sensitivity group instructor and teaching assistant in the Black American Studies Program as well as the first university graduate in that area of study. He published a manual entitled *Writing*, which was sponsored through the auspices of School District 23 in Brooklyn, New York. Each New York City school district was invited to implement it into their instructional programs. Consequently, Eric was commissioned to develop a writing curriculum for the city of New York by then Chancellor of Education Anthony Alvarado. His school-based administration and supervision experience took place in the form of principal (middle school and elementary school), assistant principal (elementary and middle school), and administrative assistant (elementary school). On the school district level, he served as reading and writing coordinator, test administration coordinator, professional development coordinator for testing, and Chief Placement officer for special education. On the central Department of Education level, he served as a test liaison to districts and school improvement facilitator in multiple districts throughout New York City. Further, he has conducted sessions of workshops for superintendents, district office personnel, principals, assistant principals, teachers, and parents on test administrations, test analysis, test security, student evaluation, and student progress including formulas for assessing school-based and districtwide achievement levels in reading and math. Additionally, he was the first to receive a Bachelor of Arts degree from Southern Illinois University in Black American studies with concentrations in economics, sociology, and cultures. His studies at SIU and Columbia University Teachers College (MA, EdM, ABD) provided a scholarly foundation for his expertise in K-12 education in the areas of supervision, curriculum and instruction, student success, operations, administration, evaluation, supervision, school culture, teacher training, assessment, policy decision-making, community relations, parent involvement, and student learning. It is within this expansive base of experience and preparation that ideas and concepts in this book are presented.

CPSIA information can be obtained
at www.ICGtesting.com
Printed in the USA
BVHW082232150721
611403BV00003B/6

9 781637 104859